Sky Above the Temple

June 5, 2021

Sky Above the Temple

*To Anna—
with gratitude
and best wishes!*

by
David D. Horowitz

David D. Horowitz

Rose Alley Press
Seattle, Washington

Published in the United States of America by Rose Alley Press

For information, please contact the publisher:

Rose Alley Press
David D. Horowitz, President
4203 Brooklyn Avenue NE, #103A
Seattle, WA 98105-5911
Telephone: 206-633-2725
E-mail: rosealleypress@juno.com
URL: www.rosealleypress.com

The author gratefully acknowledges the following poems in this book first appeared, or will appear, in the following publications:

Candelabrum: "Shields," "Green Shoot from the Funeral," "Lasting," "Legion," "Death of the Middle Ages," "Vase"
www.davejarecki.com/blog: "Knowledge"
The Lyric: "So Can," "Harbor," "Culture," "There—Can You See It?," "Oh, Fame!"
www.protestpoems.org: "Some Talk Is *Not* Cheap," "River"
Quill and Parchment: "October 10th" (published as "October 1st")
Shot Glass Journal: "April Alley"
The Smoking Poet: "Quake," "The Prince"
Unfolding Leadership, www.unfoldingleadership.com: "Wall Street, 2008"
Village Wit: "Browser," "Mistakes," "Education," "Morality," "Not for Tyrants," "Nature"
We Remember Michael Dublè (Seattle: Gazoobi Tales, 2010): "Blessing"

ISBN 978-0-9745024-9-6

Cover image: "Trajan Temple in ancient city of Pergamon, Turkey," Stock Photo #6263150, 123rf.com. Photographer: Olena Talberg. Usage rights were bought from 123rf.com.

Printed in the United States of America

CONTENTS

Sky Above the Temple

Person

A week of bicker, haggle, overload
Annoyance, when your pencil snaps
And pen stubs ink and gossip yaps
And you can't find the street to river road:
Then silence, yoga, prayer, and empathy,
To recognize a *person* in an "enemy."

Browser

—*for Amber, Sparks, & Butch*

Used bookstore?—cozy range for this gray tabby.
In here guests hush, though normally gabby.
They hunt their literary prey—pause, peruse,
Peek, sample, deepen—and let me lick, yawn, snooze
In sun as traffic slides past window. Here
A subject-ordered world calms human fear
And cultivates reflection. Stroke my fur
And browse to later Mozart overture
And sip some chamomile tea. Tabby
Lives here for you—quiet, a little flabby,
But quite content. You've petted me, mewed "Cute"
And "What's its name?" to *The Magic Flute*
And *Don Giovanni*. Now, don't get blabby.
Browse, read, buy. Help the owner, or he'll lose
His lease, and I will lose my spot to snooze.
So buy that book, and help a working tabby.

Place for Pages

You'd browse, then buy a bargain paperback.
Now *CLOSED*, front window smashed to spider web of crack,
Used bookstore morphs into graffiti canvass
For those adjacent to the pricey campus.
I'm thrilled a soup-and-sandwich shop arrives
There soon, won't mirror nearby joints and dives.
I miss the books, though, and "Beret," the tabby
Who strolled the aisles. What's to be's to be.

What better salad, though, than bookstore's discount rack?

CD Shop, RIP

I often buy CDs here. They still stock
The latest from my local indie hero,
And World Beat, Hip Hop, country, jazz, Baroque,
CDs from every group at Woodstock
To greatest hits of Laura Nyro,
Rough Guides to European, Asian folk:
A glorious emporium of tone
And pitch. It liquidates in days.
Scream latest number ones or, loser, leave
The premises, replaced by profit's clone.
Make money, sure: I'll help. Glitz up displays:
I understand. Aspire and achieve:
Of course. But make a fortune *now*—or *scram*?!
No. Wine should age in cooper's cask. A rose
Loves nourished earth. Sweet bread must bake at just
The *right* heat. Rush, push, hustle, threaten, ram,
Shout, bellow—how to ruin culture; close
The songbook; damage custom, trade, and trust.

I'll find a store that helps a local band
And offers expertise, but how long
Can it sell skuffs at two for five,
Not charge for searches—any label, brand—
Advise a friend about a group or song,
Keep in remainder bin a *Motown Live*,
Hank Williams, Mozart's late sonatas? One
More week, it seems. Then silence, dust, and lock.

Morality

X smokes. Y drinks. Z Webcam strips. A cracks
His knuckles. B combs his nose hair. C plays
The horses twice a month. D devours
A box of chocolate truffles. E can gaze
At TV soap operas for twelve straight hours.
F crosswords nights. G always stains his slacks
At work. H works and works and won't relax.
I purchases CDs, CDs, CDs.
J smokes, drinks, and slurps his Diet Cokes.
K, L, M, N, O, P, and all the V's
Show something—they can't stop telling jokes
Or taking baths or railing on some tax
Or scarfing peanut butter sandwiches with lemon slices
Or Caesar dressing or banana peel
Or…something. Most indulge, forgive such vices,
And, often, rightly.
                              Don't murder, rape, or steal.

Stride and Stretch

Far headlights trickle on the bridge
Across the lake, and work week starts.
Clouds veil the quarter moon but stars
Still spread their silence to the brim

Of dawn. Alarm exploded sleep,
And shower rinsed the snooze from heart.
Rest yields now to statistic-smart
Ambition, leisure to a sleet

Of task. While deadline dictates stride
And scandal taints a profit, wage
Funds family, and workday's cage
Frees evening to returning ride

Across the lake to leisure's stretch,
Hard thoughts in easy chair, a break
Repairing damage. Then awake:
Work tasks. Once home, though—sing, write, sketch.

Dusk Sigh

As daytime nestles into harbor, lake
And bay purr opal lullaby of wave
Calmrippling underneath a sailboat wake
And freighter, hull as massive as a cave.

Bridged traffic sparklehurries waterfront
And emberflows to homes in neighborhoods,
The shores of respite. Now, release the brunt
Of task, and breathe fresh leisure. Stroll near woods

And lake. Dusk fills its sails with slow, wakes
Cool meadowsilence. Contrail fans its plume,
And cirrus crimson in horizon's lakes.
Today: deceit, corruption's hidden room,

Ambition's shrug accepting bribe. Now, breathe
Past sigh, and somehow hope, not merely seethe.

Loyal Community

—USA, 2008

"Show loyalty!" the governor exhorts.
"Say nothing, understand?!" as he extorts
Campaign donations, bribes, and thwarts
Refusers. Big state agencies and local courts,
State legislature, businesses, all sorts
Of friends and cronies at the docks and ports,
And funders of arenas, sports:
All praise the governor, who then escorts
The biggest payers through his back door.

"I won't resign, did nothing wrong!" he snorts.

"I work for everyone!" Indeed, governor.

To Win Close Elections

You don't need millions of bucks or backers—
Just several sharp computer hackers.

Culture

And opposite the freeway traffic jam
Clouds drift pastel through turquoise and defy
The tinder tempers of a deadlined day,
Snafu and snarl and snit. The twilight sky
Glows opal pearly peach, flows *am*,
Not *must become*, nor storms at each delay.
We wait for justice, love, respect, or praise;
Most earn in bits. The overlooked and undermined,
Betrayed or thwarted, learn to persevere,
Excel for handshake and a modest raise,
As face on grinning team, someone still kind
Because of prayed-for patience. Deadlines near;
She'll do the job again, earn pay and thanks
Yet stay another name within the ranks.

Thriving Enterprise

Despite her argument with husband late last night,
Teen smoking pot and barely earning C's,
Pet basset with another case of fleas,
And daughter dawdling over social network site;
Despite the cancellation of her favorite show,
More price hikes at the market, less
Spare cash for school supplies and prom dress,
New car, iPod, and braces; and despite stubbed toe
And macaroni recipe that failed to thrill,
She's here at work today—to file, fax,
Call, photocopy, staple, proofread. She can fix
A cranky printer, calm a nervous ego, chill
Dessert, dash out for ham-and-Swiss on rye
At five p.m. to feed a busy boss.
She'll simply have to catch a later bus.
She'll offer for the bake sale apple pie
And blouses for the clothing drive. "I eat,
Have work. My best friend? Jobless seven months.
So call me lucky. I went through that once."

World, note: her kindness helps her firm compete.

M – F

I

She calculates through spreadsheet and database
And sips at mocha grande, turns down tune
On headphones, settles in for afternoon
Of task—and longing for adoring face.

II

With suit and high heels off, she sits in blouse and jeans
And leopard-spotted slippers, scans the database
And photocopies, staples, mutters at machines
And blesses tech support, her supervisor's grace.

III

She knows! She lost the letter, has her flaws and failings
And always flubs—but why insult her, shred her feelings?!

IV

Okay: the bookstore gift card, rose bouquet,
And concert tickets help. She'll stay.

V

It's Friday! Tasks must be done by five
Or she'll be…well, not really "skinned alive"
And yet…. She mirrors supervisor's drive.

Place

Computer eyestrain headaches, paper cuts,
Cramped lower back, and carpal tunnel throb.
My desk: a stack of stacks and paper cups
Of paper clips or cold beige coffee. Job:
I need your tasks. You keep me off the skids
Of alcoholic alleyways, their brick
Cliff sky and puddles. You supply my kids
And pay my bills. Sometimes you make me sick
Of life, yet ruts provide some comfort, grooves
I needn't plow anew each week. My chums
Commiserate and cheer. There's lakes and groves
Each month on calendar. There's tea and Tums
For tension, projects focusing each sprawling day,
My office window over sunny silver bay.

Work-Day Poet

With boxes of a dozen different teas,
With cocoa packets, sugar substitutes
And paper towels, with all amenities
Of office kitchen, I fill cabinets
And cupboards. I wipe down each countertop,
Restock the conference rooms with tape and tacks
And tabs, pins, pens. At five p.m. I stop
And re-emerge within, past grinning tact.
My homeward bus soon speeds up freeway ramp,
And I release the day that has been,
Anticipating friends and food and lamp
For reading. Still, I smell of jasmine.

Dusk Gull

Lamps nestle into neighborhoods and glow
Like luminescent golden berries.
In distant sky float gulls; a crow
Jeers nearer by, while in the bay, two ferries
Float black silence; range silhouette serries
Horizon's rosy shadow, evening
And settling traffic's echo. Dusk can bring
Such calm ambition pauses, gazes out its window,
And, for a second, feels nothing
But blessing candlequiet lamps, clouds towing sky
To night, more work, the faintest gull cry.

To a Gull

You wheel among the corporate suites
Above the traffic-crowded streets
Beside the misty golden-gray
Of harbor, tucked within the bay.
Your wings interpret currents, steer
Your impulse through the winds. You jeer
The car horns, as you glide and lap
A block of afternoon and loop
Horizon, playful as an otter.
Let stars emerge, lamps bloom another
Dusk, you still cry and glide and flap.

Passion

It's eight p.m. The coffee maker brews
Fresh Starbucks, trickling up the site gauge. News
Whispers from one office; computer printer drones
In other. Several brokers chat on telephones;
One jokes, forks teriyaki to his mouth
From Styrofoam container, clicks his mouse
On dollared numbers, mumbles, thanks his friend
For her advice, and promises call back.
Soon, coffee, fresh. He craves it blazing black.
Twelve-hour day twists every hour, end
Not even close. Captivity like this
Evolves to comfort. He might even miss
Tie-loosened office nights. Here one can lose
Oneself in work, as French Roast trickles, brews.

Importance

Beyond the billion-dollar business deal;
The strike and boycott, march and rally;
The classes, tests, and grades; the banquet meal;
Award and contest; shopping mall in valley
And highrises downtown; convention speech
And barroom boast; the screaming stadium
And praying pews; the freeway's headlit speed,
Then jams and horns; jobs' sprint, sweat, tedium;
The storewide sale and bargain-clutching crowds…

Dawn's golden haze, dusk's gray-magenta clouds,
A ferry vanishing past tuft of bluff
And barely sparkling bridge above the bay
By coast-road glitter, under contrail fluff
Disintegrating into darkness, day
Receding into starlight, lamps, signs, meals,
And sleepiness. Tomorrow, more big deals.

Yawn at Dawn

He showers, shaves, and dresses (slacks-and-sweater look);
Downs orange juice, then bowl of wheat-flake cereal;
Then strides to bus stop on the main arterial
And waits for his express with crowds and latest book,

A thriller. Dawn, beyond the bay, peeks golden spark
Between two peaks, then rises slowly from the lake
To warm emerging hurry, yawning, half-awake.
The full moon's coin glows ghost of fading dark

And shadow of the disappearing lamps,
Receiving skyline, filling freeway ramps.
The carpools, buses, ferries, trains all land
Downtown. He grins and sighs: all goes as planned.

He longs for some explosion
Of his routine, this gray erosion.

The Good Life

Not two hundred grand a year,
Not ten-room, two-car ranch house near
Suburban lake and mall and school.
Not dishwasher and swimming pool,
Professional prestige and fame
And Renoir print in gilded frame
And wife on PTA who bakes
Prize-winning marble coffee cakes.

That life's all right. He doesn't hate
The climbing class. He knows the freight
Of poverty for art and knows
Why some prefer the simple prose
Of 8-to-5. It's just that he
Needs pen and paper, liberty
And green imagination,
Quicksilver conversation
More than he craves some wide-screen television
Or VCR. Let derision
Advise and mock. Again, he'll need
Pen, paper, freedom, to write and read.

Selling

Each song must scintillate into a hit.
Your books must start a riot at the stores
And sell in numbers reaching to the stars.
Your name must follow phrase like "famous wit"
Or "world-renowned authority." Town halls,
Arenas have to fill to hear you speak.
Your interviews must kindle purchase, spike
An online retail boom and pack the malls.
So, grow outrageous to compete, to win
And shine…

        My art must stay well crafted, deep—
Or toss it on a rubbish heap.

ARTISTIC TRIUMPH

Troubadour

Commit yourself to honesty and art?
Construct a monastery in your heart
In which to light a candle—listen
To it, as fame and money glisten.

Finish

Your writing here improves. Though good,
It needs some finish, so "sand the wood."

Vital

Your poems—sweet despite your strain and stress,
Fresh cider squeezed from circumstance's press.

Poetry Citizen

He'll buy your book, attend your reading, offer vibe
Of love, encouragement, support—and never as a bribe.

Juice

I juice five hundred words of prose to ten
Of verse—their essence, tone.

Treatment

Your essay? Keep it pithy, brief.
First, trim the fat. Then prime the beef.

Pro

He reads and knows: her poem's good. He can't
Outdo her with a simple rhyme or rant.
Sharp imagery, distinctive verbs, line breaks
Quadrupling meaning—here is practiced skill.
His heart must close its eyes. He wants to kill
Himself or her, to never write again,
To stab a brick wall with his favorite pen,
To write the greatest poem ever. Yet,
He sighs and yawns, and reads again, and, yes,
Her poem's excellent, and he, professor
And expert critic, composed a lesser
Piece. So—he swears he'll offer help. They'll find
Some journals for her verse. He knows how fakes
Attack and self-deceive while, undermined,
Their victims seethe, so he, a second-rater,
Must, must, for poetry assist a greater.

Champion

A prison of his pettiness, a jail
Of jealousy, his heart could never grin
For others' talent. He would pray they fail,
Allowing him to claim he's champion.

Who wins when envy roots for peers to flop,
And who can make such meanness stop?

Greatness

Behind congratulation's grin
Shines envy's dagger. Who doesn't win
Strokes blade—yet your kind words don't flare
Sarcastic parry, not mere air
Or hustle. Your eyes glisten joy
For others, spurning pious ploy.
Secure in your achievement, you
Use knife to pare your own words: few,
Precise, and honest. Celebrate
Such generosity! You're great!

98 Mph

Talk, dream, imagine your success. Great!
    Now snare the scorching liner;
    Smack the darting slider;
And score, catcher walling off home plate.

Oh, Fame!

Can you endure ten cameras in your face
Demanding controversy, filming every wart
And worry, every stress, each stretch line, stare
And scowl at stupid question, bit of bare
Pain? Stroll for groceries, stride into court,
Hug lover—there are cameras every place
And prods to answer dirt hunt's probes: the maid
Who swears you snort cocaine, chauffeur who claims
You are that orphan's parent! This barrage
Will hound you out your door or from garage,
At party, theater, concert. Certain names,
Like yours, sell copies, and rent must be paid.
So, in the maelstrom, hone and polish craft,
And try to stay humane, as you're photographed.

❀   ❀   ❀

Final Show

Well, we won't perform
These songs again. Twelve years of harmony
And argument, of touring through a swarm
Of discord, revelry and rivalry
And reconciliation. Twelve years drop
Into a local music footnote, list
Of bands from then to then. You were a flop?
Soon, no one knows or cares. Big hit? Just missed?
Our molecule of influence will fade.
I'll sing tonight, and some will cry and whine,
Regret the songs that were or weren't played
By "overrated group in long decline,"
By "local icons with large following."
Sound check. Ready. Sing.

Idol

When fame diminishes, esteem might shout
And sulk, insist and rant—because self-doubt
Infects your blood. What cure? You watch your dream
Entangle songs in lawsuits, feuds. Fans scream
For younger idols. Your name and rise now mean
Five oldies hits for some eternal teen.

Immortality

Our greatest hits, our signature "sweet sound"
Evolved just jamming nights. We'd hang around

With lots of cheap red wine and packs of smokes
In someone's basement. Songs can start as jokes.

The Immortals

This pebble might outlast the tallest tower.
Soft stone might reach a later hour
Than hardest human bone, and yet we dream
Of immortality through verse,
Outlasted by the phrases, "*Carpe diem*,"
"What does that mean?," and "Send a hearse."

#1

Addicted to applause, he'd farce a friend
And spray paint reputations, gag and gab
And mug and mock, obsess about a trend,
Betray to please. When he's on stage, he'll grab
And clutch the mic: His Moment (cannot end)!

Patronage

The royal spies watch all I do—to test
    My loyalty. They offer silken robes
    And jars of cinnamon and spinning globes.
They promise publication in the best

And most prestigious places—if, oh, if
    I merely could revise. His Majesty
    Seeks more reciprocation for his tea
And brandy, coins and gems—make verse a gift

To benefactors. Touch up here or pare
    A phrase from sonnets, odes, and elegies,
    My panegyrics falling to their knees
To praise my king. A phrase, yes, here and there

Reflecting preferences that vary
A mote from his. They make him wary.
Well, I will try to think, write, and behave….

He does not want a poet but a slave!

Sketch

Hiatus, respite, interlude, a break:
I doodle possibilities. I sketch,
Conjecture, wonder. Mind can reawake
From overwork. I toss ideas and fetch
Responses, breathe new leisure, stroll
Museums. Ambition hibernates from goal,
And schedule nestles into doable.

Not dreaming ocean, still I swim in lake.
Not flinging fastballs, I love playing catch.

Tower Climb

By Wednesday, I have climbed the mountain crest,
The Great Divide between the east and west
Of Work Week Range, and feeling grateful, blest,
Reenergized, I manage all the rest—
The filing, typing, copying—unstressed
Enough to love my job. It lets me strum
And sculpt and sketch, not beg for rag and crumb.

Golden Silver

I might sleep late, jot down the wrong address,
Mistake the sugar for the salt,
Clean room but drop so much I leave a mess,
Or compliment but actually insult.
I might provide too many facts, confuse
When clarifying, stain with phrase,
Misquote or misdirect, or hide then lose,
Or turn a dial far too far and freeze
Instead of thaw. I *learn*, though—silver lining
That curbs my errors, judgments, whining.

AND IF YOU TEACH

Buzz, Buzz

Flies, gnats, mosquitoes buzz or bite and pester,
And yet I do my work, let the buggers fester!

Oh, Well

The gossip relishes my every flaw and gaffe
And whispers soot. I yawn and laugh.

Tolerance

We can't know truth or goodness, so I fear
Intolerance. You think you're right? Get out of here!

Decision of a Sort

It's indeterminate. We can't be sure
Or know. And yet—through decision we mature.

Qualification

"Compassion!" your professors preach at school.
And I'll add: strength. That is "strong," not cruel.

Mirage?

You smirk and glance away when friends bless hope, renewal.
Okay: on road, naïvete might believe mirage. Hope still is fuel.

So Can

Religious faith can make one preachy
But so can love of Marx or Nietzsche.

To Sanctimony

We all feel *some* bias
So don't get *too* pious.

Education

Bump, stumble, drop, forget—but learn;
And if you teach, recall your gaffes
Before you castigate or spurn
Or satirize for easy laughs.

❋   ❋   ❋

SPILLS—AND SPILLS AVOIDED

Mistakes

He slips, spills—sugar, creamer, coffee cover half the floor!
He sighs, daubs rags, wipes, scrubs.... It's cleaner than before!

Effort and Planning

He scrubbed, tore, rubbed, swore he'd erase that spot
And scrubbed more—yet, the messier it got.

Most Essential Part

Bills, glitches, breakdowns, gaffes, betrayals barrage
Me. Problems? Challenges in camouflage!

Of a Prize Winner

You don't lounge or celebrate, boast or bask.
You finish your next task.

❀   ❀   ❀

Resetting

With evening symphony and snack and stroll
You balance workload and achieve your goal.
Now rest. Stars clarify the silence. Moon
Sighs sheath of cloud. Eternity—not *hurry, soon*—
Slows mind to pace of breeze and sky. Reset
Your pace to *calm*. No person is an island, yet
All need one. There one reads, strolls, listens. Bend
And stretch, relax alone; you'll be a better friend.

Good Cause

One, *one* more task, a *single* chore, I'll snap!
The poor need better food; the world needs peace;
The bathroom wall needs off-white paint; I need release
To cleanse and calm my blood. I need a snack
Of leisure. Then, I might come back
To offer help and expertise—
But now? One more demand, I'll crack!

Counterpoint

I chip at list of tasks, drill into chores,
And charge across responsibilities
As budgets wobble, expectation soars,
And leisure time contracts. Ambition's fees

Pour pressure onto hope. So I retreat
To yoga mat, to hillside stroll, to book
And evening nap. Let fans praise every feat.
I'm flesh and flaw, stubbed toe and aching back,

A tantrum here, cold silence there, some one
To idolize, then blame. I need my friends
Who let me bump and burp and fail—and run
Free, who don't plot for favors or depend

On fantasies of me. I need a stroll
And song to hum, as well as plan and goal.

Peaceful Pulse

—for massage therapists

I loosen stress's grip, unlock the grin
Trapped inside task, the grit
Of strain and overwork.
Pain gremlins giggle soreness, stiffen world
To schedule, lists of chores
And disappointments over wealth and wars
And love. Breathe back to balance, pulse. Often
Massage helps strengthen—*and* soften.

Leisure

Reflect, relax. Now, saunter garden path.
Read, sketch, converse in wicker rocking chair.
No dash through shower. Linger in a bath.
No cramming lunch. Delve taste. Wake spice. Prepare
A meal and share it. Kiss, confide, and deepen.

Now, you return to work, let dawn seep in.

Still Searching

He never mocks another's love, though immature,
Misguided, hyperbolic, or impure.
He might refuse, might not respond, but never mock.
His offered roses once were laughing-stock,
His ode on card mere fodder for recycle bin,
His open heart occasion for a grin.
He might refuse, might not respond, might not unlock,
But never tease admirer's bad luck
Or judgment, misled searching for a cure.

Seeing the Thorns

When young, he would have hollered blame; he'd lash
At *women, weakness, wasted months*. Now, he sighs,
Knows unseen thorns might scratch, can empathize
When worry drops a vase, when drivers crash
Despite precaution; lovers, so complex
Their situation, tangle up in promises
And possibilities, careers, and sex,
Ambition's thrusts, pain's silences.
Oh, for a moment hug and kiss might cure
When love itself might not endure.

IN SEARCH OF CLICK

The Lady and the Courtier

Have you found greater beauty and not missed
Me? Is your claim to love mere pretty story?
My answer, madam: no people in the category
"More beautiful than you" exist.

In Love

Love—rose you sniff as air
When only air is there.

Manhood

He knows her glances, every kind of grin,
Each sort of silence. He walks inside her skin
And tenses like her heart, can just begin
To love, not boast about a score or win.

Couplet

Let pettiness nitpick and pressure bicker,
Stress snap. He'll sigh and praise, remain her backer.

Limits

Look: stay away from me! Don't go! She might
Think both. He cannot do both. Day's not night.

She Considers

He thinks he loves me, doesn't know I snore
And burp, that I hate cooking, yet I grab
The midnight inch-thick cheddar sandwich or
Gulp scotch-and-soda with my headache tab.

I'm rude. I can be. Told off innocence
A thousand unfair times, and I'll nab
A freebie. I can smirk at kindness, wince
At honesty, defy and sneer. I'll stab

At others' self-esteem. I'll…help and praise
Sometimes. I love red roses, faintest stars,
A city lake at night—reflections blaze
Their cherry and vanilla. And bookstores:

I'd live there! So, I'm touched and sad and tough.
His roses?—way too much. Or, not enough.

Click

He didn't "win her." Rather, they strode and strolled
The same path, and each craved a hand to hold.

Epithalamion

My heart can pound a tantrum; I'm afraid
Of long commitments; and my sleeves are frayed,
Yet here's the golden wedding ring. Though flawed
A million crazy ways, I'm not a fraud.

Guide

She phrases honesty like tact
And guides to peace through thorny fact.
Her smile heals rejection's bruise
Yet never overpromises. She cues,
Not condescends. Her hands might take
Your rose, refuse your love, yet make
You see her side. And here's your rose
Back. *Watch out for the thorns*, she'll close.

Stings

Her heart remembers weeping—his betrayal
Still stings her blood. *Will this one also fail?*
She wonders of her newest love. His eyes
Blaze loyalty—but so can clever lies.

Vase

He rubs his finger on her window sill—there's dust
He hadn't seen before, and soon mistrust
Emerges, mingling with his warmth and lust.
Her vase of roses, though, still shows her heart
Sky-reaching, lucent. Flaws, like flesh, stay part
Of passion. After rain, some moisture might yield rust.

Understatement

I'd call you treasure, blessing, joy,
Yet that could pressure and annoy,
And honey, rose, and blossom—praise
Too redolent of verse clichés
Could merely cloy. My silence, then,
Will echo my appreciation.

To Distraction

Love agitates the pulse, scorches blood,
And singes hope. I cannot eat, barely breathe.
I chatter hope to self in solitude.
I swoon through daily task and, evenings, seethe
Or stroll around my dream. Elate and brood
And sigh, drink memory, parch. Nothing soothes.

Woo-Woo

Her beauty tempts. First prize: he gets to kiss
Her lips but also must endure her hiss,
Sarcastic jabs, and knock-out blows. He serves
Her whims to win, inflames his blood and nerves,
Shines. Now, he steadies flame but cools his steel
In whiskey, hardens. He might win, curse yet kneel.

Peak of Love

You're *not* a peak I have to scale,
A game I have to win, a wall
I have to batter down, a sale
I have to make, resistant will
I have to break, nor golden dawn
I must adore. Say *No*? I'm gone.

Surprise Ending

She dumps and snubs him. Now she waits
To see how he retaliates.
He praises her to friends, leaves her alone.
She knows retaliation's looming. Love
Abandoned breeds abuse. He must be petty.
He praises her to friends, seeks no one's pity.
She knows retaliation's stalking. Men
Leer, pester, cling, avenge. They always mean
Slapped hopes. She knows retaliation, ends
All contact. He accepts it, praises her to friends.

No Mirage

This week: an earthquake, hurricane, and flooding,
Explosions, shootings, stabbings, a barrage
Of bloodshed, weeping sighs, and no mirage,
And there: two lovers kiss, romance budding.

❀   ❀   ❀

SAFETY?

Anything But

He'll slap and kick, chase, holler, stalk, and bruise,
And call it part of love: "What!? *Me* abuse!?"

Reality

Five months from marriage smooch to murder.
And he *swore* he'd never hurt her.
And now he shoots himself, as well,
In parking lot of Honeymoon Hotel.
He'd acted on TV, rehearsed
For that, but this scene had to be a first.
"Reality TV," indeed.
On nightly news, two dead.

One Wrong Word

*Police Team Hunts for Man Who Shoots, Kills
Ex-Wife, Three Children.* Yes, the headline chills:
Our country's fourth such tale this week. Stress, bills,
Job loss, affair perhaps, and booze and pills,
Some in-law's frowning judgment, all the ills
Of marriage. And, man's heart—a pointing gun
Behind grin's greeting, bayonet to guts,
Resentment's vengeance. One wrong word: stress spills,
Blasts "ex"—and why?—and kids: six, four, and one.

For a Woman Stabbed to Death by Her Husband

He doesn't want a wife. He wants a slave.
And now she's free of him—and in her grave.

Sanguine

Our fierce
Blood ablaze to pummel, plunder, pierce

Can recognize mistake, atone for sin;
Can contemplate dusk's sheathy saffron sun

And rosy cirrus filament, the star
That bobbles in the evening pond; can stir

To help a wounded friend, the stranger stunned
By earthquake, battle, random shooting. Stained

Violent, our minds attempt to cleanse
With prayer and ritual and praise of friends,

And yet blood clings to rage. We need to vent
And pray we haven't killed once rage feels spent.

❀   ❀   ❀

GUMSPOT

There

Wrong glance can get you shot here. Night streets
Bark silence, slink shadow, chafe mean streaks.
Pride brawls. Now, in gutter, last blood streams.
Around the corpse—no one. Street lamp gleams.

Scars

That street? Each sidewalk gumspot
Could mark where there's been gunshot.

Green Shoot from the Funeral

Gang members shot to death a rival
A week ago. These streets are tribal,
Protection needed even for the tough.
Here, some will kill to guard an inch of turf.

At funeral—some sniffles, tears, and mumbling sound
Of prayer. And mention, not of turf, but common ground.

❀   ❀   ❀

Not on TV

He's barricaded, trapped behind his fear,
Might try to shoot his way to happiness,
Resenting claims that he should persevere,
When he's done so, and *No one could care less.*

Divorce and bankruptcy both loom. He'll glare,
Lash hatred hearing his wife's name and scowl
When he sees business partner's picture. Where
Is help, and where are they? Both kids at school

Raise hands and boast their "Two plus two is four!"
Now Papa bullets up his pistol, dreams
Of visiting his wife to tie the score,
But waits, imagining their children's screams.

He unloads bullets, pistol gleaming table,
And notes TV: a murder scene on cable.

He puts the pistol back in table drawer.

Human

I'm just a piece of earth. I breathe and walk and eat,
Sweat, sniff, consider, measure, doubt, absorb, excrete,
And marvel and exalt. I'm just a piece of earth,
Rinse dust from hands. Though king or peasant, serf or earl,
I bleed. My heart is soft. I rage, I weep, I irk,
I pray. And wonder: am I *just* a piece of earth?

Wall Street, 2008

Grin's promise looted trust and hustled many
Gilt scams on fun's installment plan,
Then loaded trust into its minivan
But dropped nicked dime and tarnished penny,
Torn five. Our firm now wobbles, teeters.
I scour want ads, hunt for honest leaders.

Resting the Engine

Till weekday four a.m. he's scooting, sleeps
A blip. On weekend, though, he'll hibernate
In snooze, doze daytime like eternal night.
Yes, when he sleeps at last—it's like *collapse*.

Silhouette

I

Magenta-crimson cirrus over mountains' silhouettes
Back goldglow punchcard skyscrapers—ambition's minarets.

II

Express bus whisks. High-rises loom in rose-
Blue luminance. Soon: cubicles in rows.

The Biz

Divorces and affairs, addiction
To heroin, the bottle—I like its promise!

Hawk scandal: even verge on fiction,
But shock 'em! Recovery's the premise.

Art legend rises, falls—*returns*! This sells:
Morality tale, with pics. Fame's private hells—
I smell a movie deal. Rich dramas!

STIR THE STEW

Crunch!

A cracker *cracks*. Flat, dry, with sesame
Or poppyseeds or plain, round, square, rice, wheat,
Or rye, triangular or starry, sweet
Or salty. Smear with salmon spread or Brie
Or top with strip of Swiss or cheddar. Crunch!
And crunch! Leave room for lunch!

Versatility

In you I boil water; heat my soup;
Rewarm the stew for hungry group;
Stir pasta sauce; mix honey in my oats;
Melt butter; thicken gravy for its boats;
Store, marinate, and sear. What a lot
Of uses for a little metal pot!

Room

That fridge!—so stuffed, and with spare space so thin
You need a crowbar to cram a carrot in!

❁   ❁   ❁

NESTS

Harbor

Put into harbor, gale-battered vessel.
We will restock, repaint. You can nestle.

Sunshower

You stay serene and kind despite your strain:
A double rainbow through the blue sky rain!

Friends

Friends, like Mohave drizzle—rare
Yet real: that cactus pear.

Tinge

The bay's perimeter a glimmer, twilight blurs
The neighborhoods, except for spires, Douglas firs,
And streetlamps. Rouge-magenta cirrus fringe
Dims. Freeways brighten underneath a tinge
Of moon, disintegrating contrail, stars
Suggesting silence over ocean roar of cars.

✹   ✹   ✹

Dot

They pray you fail; they grin their plot
And mumble self-embrace. They pray you quit.

Stream flows past bluff and hill, and star stays lit
And looks no larger than a dot.

They want to be the stars. How dare you thrive?!
They grin a trap. You shine. Let them connive.

Required Skill

One's eyes, one's mouth, the lines upon one's face
Convey dislike, suspicion, or embrace.
Deceit will mask, though. You must learn to read
Pause, tic, off-glance if you want to lead.

Picturesque

The meadow, from a distance: sunny, green.
Up close: steel gate, barbed wire fence, fine screen
At checkpoint, rifle-stroking men and fierce-eyed teen.

From the Highest Tower

They scratch, claw, bite, yet not overtly fight
Me yet. Threats nibble at the foot
Of fame. They scout all weakness and thrust
And pry, poke. I am king and trust
My soldiers' skill, and yet I pray the Lord
Resolves disputes without the sword.
Here faction undermines. There foreign troops
Prepare for battle, claim to honor truce.
I witness from the highest castle towers
Each snake try slithering through meadow flowers.
I rule—which means my sword stays sharp and sleek;
My crown aglitter; hand extended, never weak.

Tarnish

Troops swarm, cock rifles, hunt dissent, and shoot
At shadows. They might smash down door of house
To threaten, bribe and praise the rat and mouse,
Report they'd weeded out the problem's root.
Dissent, though, boils up in different town
And neighborhood. No gun can change a lie
To truth. Dissenters march, know they might die—
Wiped off—like tarnish from a crown.

PENNY JAR

Not For Tyrants

Don't *say* it?! I should cower, tremble
Lest power disapprove? Dissemble
For tyrants? No—although I do feel fear—
First guard integrity, not career.

Tyranny

Companion, mentor, friend? Their behavior
Suggests they crave a *savior*.
Flaw, lapse, indifference? Not allowed.
They want a reign without a cloud.

Loyalty

We need morality to battle sin!

Our halfback raped a woman at an inn?
Not good, but…he must play. We have to win!

To See

He sees hypocrisy—his giggle melts to grief
As kleptomania calls honesty a thief.

Uses of History

Youth's playfield tussles, bloody noses, black eyes, scars and scares
And losing scores mature his friendship voice and deepen prayers.

Fawn

It's fragile
But agile.

Festival Sales

His sales-eye clutches at the passers-by,
Who mainly want to mumble "Hi"
And "Maybe later" buy.

Success

Persists to 2, to 3, to 4 a.m.
These nights and wakes at dawn. He perseveres
To sales; promotes into publicity;
Learns, studies, and selects the gadgetry
He needs and blazes into tasks, his gears
Hot purpose. Somewhere underneath, some *them*
Spurs him, their doubts and gossip, prayers he'd fail,
Their smirking slights. He uses rage like fuel.

Loss, RIP

*Oh, no, Cubs lose: 4 - 3…*When you lose in sport
The box score is an autopsy report.

Proportion

To spread your mustard over rye and slice a garlic pickle
Small knife works better than machete, sword, or sickle.

Master

Our Master proves that he's the real Messiah!
Your Master's white silk robe—the veil of maya?

Holy War?

When he screams, "Holy war! *Jihad!*"
I see his swords and guns, not God.

Business School Commencement Address

Your basement office has been set afire;
Your bank account stands on financial wire;
Your business reels from one disastrous hire;
You must compete against each thief and liar
You *don't* know. Now: succeed. Inspire.

To an Entrepreneur

Costs rise; the market saturates; and rivals cheat.
In these conditions, you compete.
You don't complain, though, as you deplete
Resources, sleep on office cot
And feel your muscles tense to knot.
You revel in the challenge, plot
Advance, and innovate survival, down
Cold teriyaki take-out: breakfast. "Done"
Means you can rest for maybe one,
Two hours. You revel in the incomplete.

Pedagogy

You ask for strategies: *how best to teach?*
Stir conversation, not give a speech.

Sea

I want success, of course. I strive, hope, wish.
The sea, though, stretches wide. We're *all* small fish.

Bypassing Opportunity

You're hiring attack dog and cheerleader,
But I'll stay poet, citizen, and thoughtful reader.

Vacation

B sees more a mile from his home
Than C does in London, Paris, and Rome.
B sees history in trees, houses, lawns.
C notes *Montmarte*, the Forum—and yawns.

Resolve

Commitment, clarity, solution. Star
Above the storms, beyond the clouds. The spar
That stands the sail. Dissent that fells a czar.
Love's patience stroking, kissing rawest scar.

When One Does Not Know

Tough questions can require subtle
Responses. I would only muddle,
And you already sense rebuttal.
Explore the ocean. I'm a puddle.

Salmon

I thrash and pellet through cold fresh
Climb. I resist the rapids' foam
To numb persistence. Going home
I bruise the rivers, batter flesh,
Cascade and vault and reach,
Spawn, linger, death my beach.

Consistent Heat

The deluge starts with drizzle.
The fire ends in fizzle.
True passion? That can sizzle
And sizzle and sizzle…

To a Dancer

You're proof that bounce and grace can coexist,
Can dance ballet and do the twist,
Can go-go dance at local club, and yet
Next night can cabriole and pirouette.

Halleluiah

Declaim for Jesus, yell *Ave Maria*,
Exhort Allah and exalt the Sharia
Or worship a cleric from South Korea
Or North Carolina or east of Berea….

You still might ache, quote verse of love—then hate
Someone who doesn't love your verse. You might
Recite compassion, grin, and then delight
In others' failure. Appreciate

Brown leaf, gray pebble, chilly sleet-stung night
Along with sunny noon. Ignore a slight,
And help another's talent rather than deflate
Then shield with shine. Let love soak through your spite

Still staining heart, still smirking at the great
And feigning sun. The hour's always late.

Each and Every

You aim to scale that mountain peak, but just one trail
Leads there, and it ascends along a ridge.
A stumble might yield death. Dawn's opal-rouge
Glows hope. Prepare, though, every scrap, each fingernail.
Read stone like you were blind and feeling Braille.

Of Vermeer

Cream, bone, tan, beige, gold, satin, linen, silk:
Each different. Sip of wine and stream of milk
Flow, share light's silence. And pocky plaster wall
By window whispers God in all.

Blessing
—for Michael Dublè

But he might scowl, scoff, scold, ignore polite
Hello behind his shades, indoors at night,
Then sear his trumpet's jazzy streetlight
Penumbra for the poets. Trumpet, *yes,*
That smoky bourbon horn, is how he'd bless.

Statue

For winning some forgotten battle, "Colonel Reece"
Is lettered on some street signs and park monument.
Mere granite statue now, his left arm points through sleet.
His eyes stare at a "STOP" sign near a tenement;
His rear end hollers red graffiti. Would defeat
Have offered kinder fate? Still, he seems at peace.

Holiday Season Smash

The movie features dragons and giant lizards
And witches and ogres and evil wizards
And, from the Planet Zuu, a flying dog

And not a word of thoughtful dialogue.

Light and Dry

Chilled Riesling, Chardonnay—and sharpest cheddar,
Brie, Swiss, soft goat cheese, and Havarti
On imported whole-grain crackers: yummy party!

(The conversation, well, is gossip, chatter,
But sometimes I've a taste for patter.)

Blankets

Beige wool, mauve cotton, scarlet velveteen,
Patched quilt, one's coat, a shield, a sheet,
A compliment, kiss, curse, a favorite tune,
A zone of warmth, bear fur, hair shirt,
Mauve wool, beige cotton, the stars and quarter-moon.

Necklace

The bridge links neighborhoods. Friends shake each other's hands.
Clasp binds pearl necklace—not mere string now. *Band.*
The shelf holds every type of pasta sauce—so many brands!
The view from space: lined borders? Just water, land.

Control

To clutch control to prove prestige; to grin
Because appearing kind might help you win;
To paint the perfect mask to cover face
Instead of disciplining heart with grace
And empathy; to stain and then delete
The rival who can sense, detect deceit:
Such skills the world rewards. Prepare
To sharpen claws and whiten teeth and brush
New suit—and talk compassion as you crush.

Relying on Authority

One seawater-plutonium shake
To go, with one uranium cake.
I'm told they're tasty still and cannot hurt
My tummy, and they make a great dessert!

Untempted

You want attack dogs barking out your dogma. "Boy,"
You urge me, "Here's more fame! Now, sic 'em!" I will not obey.
Success?! You want me slavering for prey,
Not seeking truth and justice. You deploy
Your staff like hounds to stalk a parrot. I'm a person.
I'm off your leash. You sweeten bribes—and worsen.

Through

Yes, honesty, slip through deception's net,
Slip past harassment's scheme, slip out
Of bully's grasp, slip under tyrant's wall,
Slip from the chains that leash your legs and neck
Because you dared to question, wonder, doubt.

Still, you'd see stars from bottom of their well.

Words

"We need community!" he rails
And prays his best friend fails.

You Might Not Win, Yet

That liar, thief, and demagogue
Believes himself a demigod
When his supporters cheer and chant
For his inflammatory cant,
His winning politics.
Employ your own sly tricks?—
Or detail policies, explaining laws,
Attentive to dissent to learn of flaws.
Prefer defeat to winning lying rant.

Beyond, Nearby

The stars do not retaliate or shun
Because you say something conservative
Or liberal or plan a night of fun.
They sparkle silver distance, dots of tin-
sel patterning the black expanse of night,
And hint the outlines of a better place.
Beyond the leer of envy, sneer of spite,
They help us navigate our inner space.

✽ ✽ ✽

TACKED TO THE CALENDAR

October 1ˢᵗ

In khaki shorts Bill rakes his lawn
As Rover pants beneath the cot.
Bill sweats two pounds. Leaves, dry and brown,
Bake, mounded. "Man," Bill sighs, "it's hot!"

October 10ᵗʰ

It's only five p.m., yet poplars shadow river,
And underneath half-moon, gold-purple meadows shiver.

Thanksgiving

For most, there's football on TV, then lots of eating.
For him, a stroll: dusk streetlamps' gold-dot trail, receding.

Snowy Commute

Beneath the lamplit snowghost air, the frozen hush
Of creamcake angelfield. There's sooty slush
A block away, gray applesauce near gutters, mush
Of traffic—so-called morning rush.

March 21st

Cold migrates back to mountaintops. Stars thaw
Above the lamps and headlights. Green buds
Chirp scarlet flowers. Sunlight glitters lake.
A cherry twig, released by sparrow's claw,
Bobs first pink blossoms. Hope, despite the bugs
And rains, renews. Sun warms the seeds awake.

The Cup Half-Full

Today the rain might soak and drench.
This summer, reservoirs will quench.

April Alley

Four dumpsters and discarded box spring mattress lean
Against a chain-link fence—and oak trees green.

April 25th

The spring sky hatches, suns the afternoon
To opal dusk. Now, cirrus sheathes the moon.
Jet contrail dissipates to gray fluff. First
Stars mirror points of lamps, not crystal frost.

Spring Midnight

Gray cloud sheath blurs full moon in sky of veils.
The freeway's lamplights sparkle, piercing distance
And linking hillsides. Lamps' even intervals
And silent vehicles—sleep's pulse, life's persistence.

Summer Note

A swallow strafes and chitters emerald pond ducks float.
Jet's contrail pierces opal dusk beyond a leisure boat.
Sweet summer—nature blossoms song, and I can shed my coat.

In Seattle

There?—Eighty-five degrees, white sun, and hurricanes
In August. Here?—Blue breaks from gray, cool rains.

Fresh Daily

Dawn holds its breath: a hint
Of red begins to tint
Sky. Pine, fir, cedar print
Branches, serried as mint.

Time Lapse

Sun vanishes—from orange-amber
Sphere to a single ember.

Deep Breath

Horizon's smoky swirl shawls peaks
    And foreground hilltop spruce and pine.
Dusk hues—maroon and scarlet, peach,
    Flame, golden-gray—bouquet like wine.

This slower pace sighs reverie.
    One needn't brood in flat or bar.
Here nature brews recovery
    As simple as a breath or star.

Resolving

Pearl-orange distance cools to opal rose.
I hear the cornice gull and streetlamp crows
Join settling hush, resolving day to close
And effort and ambition sleep
Before once more reclimbing steep
Accomplishment with step and step and leap.

❈   ❈   ❈

Detox Center

—for massage therapists

I ease the toxins from your muscles, tease
The gremlins from your joints. I lubricate
Release. I help you sigh and compensate
For disappointment. Neck and fingers, toes
And back, I stroke. Find, feel the core
Of stress—then tenderize, restore.

Mere Weariness

For each frayed muscle, furrow
On brow and mind, I sigh and burrow.
I lengthen inhalation, stretch and stroke
My legs, arms, neck—then, through green park, stroll,
Return down lamplit streets. The soiling scrum
For wage, the sweat and soreness for a crumb
Of meaning—still I'm grateful for a goal
And job, mere weariness, not sorrow,
A home below dusk's saffron cirrus smoke.

SKYLIGHT

Dwelling

She rests on floor and gazes stars through skylight.
She dwells on God in silence, like a stylite.

Wonder Full

Let questions probe and rage. I sense that God
Detests not doubt, but slavishness and fraud.

Purification

Imams brainwashed him with clearest water
So he could study texts, then slaughter
Ten children on a school bus, five teens
In night club, and nearing voting machines
Two dozen citizens, himself—and now
Who's purer? What's new?

2007

So many corpses bloody the Euphrates
In sunlight it's a scene from Hades.

❀   ❀   ❀

Reassurance
—the king's advice

One rules by edict, fiat, and decree.
Disorder lurks and creeps. Crack down

On dissidents until they back down.
Above all: no one should be free

To threaten order. For the good
We sentinel each neighborhood.

Some Talk Is *Not* Cheap

The king dreads murmurs. Now, dissent earns jail
Or bullet in an alley, bomb through mail,
Or dagger to the heart, or enemies
Who live to make truth crawl home on its knees
And die there. Martyrs might persist. Dissent
That strong and brave don't dare call less than saint.

Seer

A king of murder and extortion
Can preach law, loyalty, proportion,
Art, culture, pride—then rape a girl and scorch
A temple, light his kingdom with the torch
Of terror. I foresaw this endless war
In stolen diamonds sparkling kingdom's core.

Options

This mule won't haul your wagon anymore.
You cut my meager rations, whipped me sore
And screamed and ranted at me, sneered and swore
And bellowed insults. I cannot ignore
This much abuse. You kick my haunch and curse
Your luck. You threaten me with holy war
And whine this hilly climb. You might change course
And mules. Yes, *you* might haul this load to store,
And I'll kick *you*. I'll bolt my hoof into your gut
And smack your neck and ears with rifle butt.
No, realist? Then pat, persuade, and kiss—not force.

River

You ban all airplay of my music, sales
Of my CDs. You stab with rumor, spy,
Harass, and stalk. Oh, power: stuff your jails
With dissidents. Denounce those who defy

Your puppetry, and ruin their careers.
You order marches of obedience;
A grinning beat, not joyful pulse; canned cheers
And cued applause; in short, ingredients,

Not art. I listen to the sparrows tweet,
The vireos and warblers, and I hear
The rainstorm, river, breezes through the street
Of elms, a woman's whispered fear

And symphony LP, and your commands.
The moment yields a melody; my blood
Tunes silence into song, despite your plans
And charts, your rumors' bullet, spear, and blade.

They boast their guns who are themselves afraid.

Expensive

I traveled risk to consequence and found
Big sales and envy's sneer; four-bedroom house
And fourteen-hour days; expensive schools
And meth-addicted daughter; handshakes, praise,
Usurpers' grins; expressways and delays;
Integrity of purifying skills
Repairing broken gadgets, moody spouse;
Promotion to big office, dinner downed
With decaf, Tums, and aspirin. I stride
And stagger forward—friendly, frosty, fried.

Thrum

Another day in power, choosing some
For raises and promotion. Yes, I see
The frowns and fury those rejected feel.
B thought he'd try a bribe; C tries to steal,
And D, who'd lauded, will not speak to me.
E blames herself and weeps. F hollers "Bum!"
And "Jerk!"
                    Sweet cat, you purr because I feed
And stroke you. Murmur purr, lick paws, snooze, thrum.
You warm, you thaw my heart—now not quite numb.

Song

No snap-on smarts, push-button truths. Wisdom's earned
By being fired, dumped, manipulated, burned,
Evicted, undermined, backstabbed, spurned.
You lose your keys, your wife, your job, your mind,
Your savings, friends, house, hair, couch, car, behind,

But not your notebooks from your attic,
Black ball-point pens which zing fanatic
And zealot. Nothing automatic
And all authentic, you are sometimes wrong
And foolish—and all the wiser in your song.

Not a Widget

I'm not a button, dial, tool, or widget.
I'm not a puppy, puppet, gadget, digit,
Machine, or cipher. I can't be plugged
Into relationships or harassed, pestered, bugged
Into a friendship or community.

I'm human. Respect complexity
Of character and love of freedom, or
Don't claim the voice of "love." You're fueling war.

SPEAR-CHIPPED URN

Legion

Today we raze and pillage, crush
   Rebellious forest tribes
   Refusing Roman bribes.

I hear an infant howling through the hush.

In the Dirt

Their soldiers plunder, pillage, rape, and burn.
Posterity will see a spear-chipped urn.

The Emperor Scoffs

You claim you'll "slash Rome's throat and break its knees"?
Barbarian: how you inveigh.
My lion Barnabas needs lunch, so please
Feel welcome to invade.

The Fall of Rome
—Fifth Century, A.D.

I level Roman towns and revel in the carnage
And ash? I'm kinder than the Romans were to Carthage.

New Ancients

*—Ugo Vetere and Chedly Klibi,
mayors of Rome and Carthage,
signed a peace treaty in 1985*

Today we praise the sheath and holster, bridge
And handshake. Hug your friend and kiss your sweetie,
And set aside eternal grudge,
For Rome and Carthage sign a treaty!

Lasting

Those golden-turquoise domes our leader built!
Those scarlet oceans—blood our leader spilt.

He died. We watch his kingdom wilt.
We're left with lots of gilt.

History Textbook

_____ the Great: king, continental unifier
(through Holy Text, spears, arrows, swords, and fire).

❁   ❁   ❁

Advice About Price

Frontiers rebel. Stuff troops in trouble zones,
And massacre the dissidents. Sear their bones.

Let no one ever dare rebel again.
Blaze threats. Show bribe. Describe new bridge. Begin

To grin, assured your puppet reins. Seize land
To cultivate. Watch all proceeds as planned,

And stab or poison any trouble. Here:
You're eagle. Show your talons—shield and spear.

Reward obedience. Negotiate
With our dealers. Every lemon, fig, and date;

Each load of salt or cinnamon; each roll
Of cloth; each silkworm on the Old Silk Road;

Each ruby, emerald, diamond—each bears price
You know. They cheat, they die. All, all field mice

Should fear the circling eagle overhead,
Should sense its shadow, which redoubles dread.

Now: govern well. And teach our helpers, too,
Such statecraft. Know: the emperor watches you.

Of Selfishness

Islanda must show all the honor due
Rome's greatness, or we'll make it rue
Its independence. It must share its wheat
And corn or turn its twilight bloody. We
Must demonstrate to rebels *costs*: their fields
In flames, their towns in ashes, shattered shields,
Snapped spears, and pointless arrows, and our crown
Atop their temples, on their coins, on gown
And robe, and governing their fears. Show some
Consideration for their gods of sun
And sea, their sports, ales, songs. But Islanda will bleed
Unless its stops its disregard for *our* need.

Thick Hides

*—of war elephants in
the ancient world*

Men urge them guzzle fire-water
To stomp around to trample, slaughter,
Pound mayhem, blood to mud, as arrows
Pour into eyes and hide. Pharaohs,
Kings, emperors: why should the elephants
Run to their deaths? They're innocents
Employed as killers. Men: take swords
And fight. Or, better: seek accords.

Imperius and Luster

I hear the infants yowl and widows wail.
I stroke my little feline's back and tail.
I note the smoke above a pillaged town.
I lie on silken pillows, full of down.
I've seen the starving murder for a crumb.
I listen to a lyre, flute, and drum.
I've ordered slaughters munching pheasant lunch
And conquered peaceful countries on a hunch.

I've prayed for peace as well as glory, and I've wept
Ten Tibers nights I haven't slept.
I weep to know the just are locked in jail.
I stroke my Luster's tummy, back, and tail.
I listen to his heartbeat warn of haste
And kiss a slave girl just below her waist.
I'm emperor of Rome, a god with furrowed brow,
A soldier and first citizen, and now

I pray for victory as well as peace
To make a city's shrill complaining cease.
I'll build new roads and aqueducts. I'll snap
My fingers and, slave, servant: bring me map
And wine, two slave girls for a chilly night.
I'm emperor of Rome. I sail the Nile
And swim the Po. I greet the rich and toss
The poor their bread and games. You pour my sauce.

I'll hold my goblet still. There. Now, we rest.
Tomorrow I begin to travel west
To dedicate a temple, battle Goths,
Plan aqueduct and bridge, defend our gods,
And study what my oracles declare
About a ram's intestines. Foreign glare
Must soon become a Roman smile. Here,
Here, Luster! Yes, you purr. Here, eat some deer.

Next month fresh Gothic corpses rot in meadows.
I'll nuzzle cat and sigh for Roman widows.

The Emperor, Grateful

My Luster's whiskers twitch; his ears perk back.
His paws detect a possible attack.
He sniffs a knife and hears the vengeful glance.
So, Luster, here's fresh trout and lamb, a snack.
You've done well. Someone else will hurl my lance.

Germania

This Roman lust for glory—conquering
The alp of their ambition, boasting ring
And corselet, sheaf of chieftains, vengeful death
For Varus, now become eternal debt
To them, or liberty to murder, rape,
And swagger every stupid little raid
Into our land. In battle we defy
Yet learn from them. We learn to unify
Most disparate tribes behind a single will.
We temper stronger spears and sharpen skill
And strategy. We ambush arrogance
Amidst the forest whisper, stab and lance
Beside the mountain stream, await their dash
Through muddy valley, while some of us kiss cash
And power, glory, luxury. I fear
For calloused hearts, as well—now grown so fierce.

Fair Trade

Rome never violates a treaty. She might stay
In fertile provinces a year or two
But not illegally. Rome needs to eat.
Fertilia Felixa offers wheat
And orchards. Rome can't live on grass and dew.
Our trade makes countries rich. We'll fill their bay;
They fill our hulls, then sing of Roman gold.

Yes, Luster? Crave something delicious?
Roast pig meat? Lamb? Lucilla! Lucius!
Fill Luster's golden saucer: fresh roast pig,
Lamb stew, and halibut—and twenty lashes
For lunch tomorrow if his portions aren't big!
And bring me Luster's diamond-studded leashes!

Okay, then. Rome respects provincial pride
And culture, power and economy.
Roads, water, and protection I'll provide.
Now let my people savor evening meal.
Let provinces yield food. It's good as sold.

Dissident

Go. Conquer territory
For Rome. Win fame and glory.
And wealth—gold, slaves, and spices.

That native still despises
Us, village torched by legions
Afraid of spies in regions

We craved. Cease. It's harder
Perhaps to trade and barter
And learn. Go. Offer native minds
A golden culture, not slaver for their silver mines.

Loyal Customer

You call me friend and colleague, ally, brother
Yet pray I die. We understand each other.
I still need dye, fruit, tea, nuts, salt, and spice.
Let's trade. I'll match your highest price.

The friendly stuff? You needn't bother.

Throne Room

He bows. Oh, let ambition ponder
And plot successes, learn to flatter
And bribe, pretend it doesn't matter,
Grin next to throne, scorn those who squander
Such chances. Lusts and lapses will emerge
This grubby, gritty glory grab.
My purple robe and silken golden garb
And ruby rings mean I will have to purge
Betrayal from our elites—as daggers jab
My throne.
               I see the grinning adder,
Nod, then stroke and calm my cat. His smoky fur
Conceals his claws: my little emperor.

Chief Adviser

Some province rumbles with revolt.
Some traitor whispers bribe. Some dolt
Insists advancement. Chieftains scheme
And bicker over trinkets, team
To filch a corselet. Some court
Crook plays poisoning for sport.
Some minister claims N is M;
He pouts such depth and wisdom
Do not crown *him* the emperor.

You, Luster?—yawn, then lick your fur.
You snooze in sunny patch on bed,
Not wonder where some Dacians dead
On battlefield stored bricks of gold.
You nibble trout and pheasant, hold
And bat and chase and rip a toy
And, doing so, provide more joy
Than chest of emeralds. Snooze, sweet cat.
Rome triumphs. Later, we can chat.

Trustworthy

Those forehead furrows on my limestone bust
I earned. An emperor learns not to trust
Praise, promises, and proof. And yet my cat,
My Luster, still proves my friend. Mew and purr
Reharmonize me. Let him chase and bat
Toys! To his golden collar, pin a pearl.

Protectors

Betrayal blesses love. Spies snoop and creep
To listen for a mouse's burp. How fine!
Now envy sets out cup of poisoned wine
And prays you quaff yourself to deepest sleep.

The pimps and princes, gossips, moralists,
And blades with alibis and presents, plots
And their protectors, tied in silken knots
Of silence. Fear reprisal from the mists

And veils and screens, the courts and counselors.
And yet—ah, Luster—furry friend, ignoring
The gossip. Nay, you find it boring!
You lick your paws. They babble. Luster purrs.

Hunters

My enemies might want to kill you, Luster. Stay
Sharp, friend. Centurions show swords, spears,
And wall of frowns and helmets. What if they
Join restless generals and disobey
Or only hear untested mumbled smears?
The tenterhooks of power, Luster. Tines
Of disapproval. Envy's stabs and sneers.
What's that?! What…oh, it's you. Your night eye shines
A star. Your purr and mew are signs
Of safety. Sharpen claws on satin couch?
My lion! Ready soldier! Yes, now catch
The rats! Stay sharp, my sword. We hunt. We're prey.

Persuasion

Join Rome, king. We could cobblestone your roads,
Raise aqueducts and marble palaces.
We could refurbish and enlarge your ports,
Sprout trade routes, and establish local courts.
Whip steeds to glory, king; win games and races
And laurel crowns, lead victory parades,
And feast on venison and lamb. So why
Wait? Oh, your chalice….
                                    Slave boy, here! More wine!

More Wine!

Let envy try to trick and trap. They bore
My toenails. I smell flattery before
They smile. Phonies make my ears snore.
I've got invasions, insurrections, mice
Who play at minister—I can't play nice
And win for Rome or listen to advice
From educated fools. I win and kill
Or lose and die. That's Rome. Crushed Hannibal.
Drill, soldier! Slave, more wine! And not that swill
You served this afternoon. And for my cat—
Fetch golden goblet, silver satin mat.
There, Luster—pheasant, trout, with side of sprat.
Tomorrow, chariots! Then, Luster, …war.

More wine!

Swords and Bracelets

—for Helvidius Priscus,
Roman senator, 1st century A.D.

Dissent retreats to crypts, caves, and villas. Ally
Myself with whom? My best friend is a spy.
The emperor knows when I burp or sigh.
Gold corselet here, gold bracelet there, false words
That testify to gods—togas can't stop swords
Or bribes or rumors fed to fearful hordes.
Well, then, we must meet in crypts and caves
And villas and, possibly, in graves.

Consequence

I soften granite, melt the ice
Of opposition. Good, not nice,
I lust and storm and weep—but not
To aid an underminer's plot.
Some think my courtesy a crust,
A cowl. Well, whom in power should I trust?
An emperor who terrorizes
Dissent? The toady who advises
The midnight dagger into honor's guts?
A senate driven underground or nuts
Or silent? I don't try to be heroic.
I speak the simple truth—some call me stoic.

You Can Approach the Emperor

Approach on knees. If I so much as wink or nod
Praetorians could slice your head off. I'm a god.
Your eyes should pray, hands plead. But I can hear complaint
Of muddy road or leaky aqueduct or thieves
At grain supply. Relate your rumors, murmur's peeves
And plots. Don't lie for gold, though. I'm a god, not a saint.

The Emperor of Rome

Stab anyone you like, and burn down any home.
Who'll defy your torch? You're emperor of Rome.

You're emperor of Rome, so poison any prince
And rape his princess. They'll feel touched and honored, since

You're emperor of Rome. Ignore dissent, though flog
And torture enemies. They'll pray to join your flock:

You're emperor of Rome. Steal any lands you like,
Sign bogus treaties, smile as you sell a lie:

You're emperor of Rome. Those swords your guards now thrust
Through *you*?! You were the emperor of Rome, and now you're dust.

Purr

You'd loot my treasury? Or would extort
And deem the cash "donation,"
And were I to refuse you'd curse the court
And plot retaliation?

You kneel and bow. You tout my wisdom, laud
My kindness, bless my future,
And offer wine and robes like I were God.
You angle for my gold? Or

Land, troops, wheat, swords, spice, quarry stone?
My lion, Barnabas, purrs
Suspicion. Barnabas tears into bone,
Drools meat. Who fawns? Princes, curs.

You grin and bow and mouth "Your Majesty."
We'll trade. I want that province.
You'll get trained troops, a tapestry,
And gold. But not my cat, prince.

Cottages and Caves

—560 A.D.

The West withdraws to cottages and caves, rooms
In hilltop monasteries, cliffside holes
And texts recalled in hearts or scrawled on tombs
Or stowed behind a wall. From ruins
We salvage fragments, chips, compassion's runes.
Text-saving caves, scorched fields and forests: homes.

Devils and Heretics

Yes, torch their huts and shacks, and smash their carts
And wagons. Rid the church of evil hearts
And errors heretics like this commit,
Whose village isn't worth the devil's spit.
Now, sharpen sword and load your arrow sheaf
And aim the crossbow at demonic chief.
Like mastiffs growl and claw and rip, and charge
Like armored stallions; pour out fire, large
As dragons! Kill the devil. Later, feast
On mead and mutton. Now: your heart's a fist!

The Prince

We might retract, but never clip, our claws.
Resentment grins, and might obey the laws,
Yet prays and digs for fatal flaws.
Its trap door drops into a dungeon—straw,
Stone, chains, and bones. You purr, sweet cat, a chord
Of love, yet you can seize a mouse with paw
And fang. I pray for peace—and wear a sword.

Hymnal

Trust vassals jostling for prestige
Who murmur plots and grin "My liege!"?

Trust spy-and-blab ambassadors
Who wait for me to hire whores

To help them and the clergy sleep?
Now, Hymnal: I can *see* you creep,

Claw silken pillows, nestle calm
Throughout the palace, purring psalm

And curling like contented globe,

Ignoring crown and purple robe.

Shields

Retreat to castle keep or suffer slaughter,
Defeat to heathen enemies.
We must withstand the Saracen marauder.
God wills it. Yet, I grant their prayers amaze,
Bewilder me. They seem to pray to God,
I guess, though swords and arrows growl in sheaths,
And boulders tense in catapults. One nod
And battle could erupt. Our hearts are shields
Against surrender. Prayer shields our hearts,
Yet now I pray a battle never starts.

Prayers

Hearts blaze like torches hissing oil
From dragon's flames that sear and broil
The enemy, whose axes, swords, and spears
Are sharper than cathedral spires.
Now prayers plead God grant victory,
And kings imagine *God's for me.*

Shhhhh…God whispers in those meadows
Of corpses under vultures' shadows,
In ditches, mud, foes' blood and hair.
Hear *them* before you mumble prayer.

Bones
—1195 A.D.

                                    Carts overturned
In ditch near thatch-and-stick huts burned
To final straw of infant's bed
And crumbs of moldy barley bread.
Stream gurgles past abandoned mill.
Weeds sprout through crop fields who will till?
Who did this? Turks and Muslims, or
Crusaders, knights returned from war,
More savage? There behind that house—
Charred sticks now—cat sprints after mouse.

Villages

—1200 A.D.

We pray for heaven's grace to warm all souls,

Seethe boiling oil through the murder holes
And sizzle arrows from the barbican
And loops in tower walls, from bartizan
And parapet. Marauders ransack, seize,
And creep though forest, execute a siege,
And spear some keep, rape hearts. Here life is war.

I dreamt last night I was an artisan,
Not knight, or that I toured as troubadour.
I first must dodge swords, arrows, boulders, coals,
Respond with death and answer to my liege.
Here life shouts battle—I wear helmet, sword,
Yet dream of women, angels, and the Lord,

Of roadways linking villages, accord
Above the moats of castles ruling hills.

History
—Genghis Khan, 1162-1227 A.D.

Genghis Khan? "Our greatest leader!"
"That butcher!" "He gave us pride and law,
Spread learning." "He would harass and beleaguer,
Then threaten, kill until you felt due awe—
In other words, a tyrant." There, reader.

How Progress Happens

The King hints bribes to urge and force alliance
Between the asps and cobras, jaguars and lions.
For this, he'll let you practice art, learn science.

Tamerlane

Was lame, loved chess, collected art, stacked skulls
In pyramids; instructed troops to sever,
Retrieve two heads of enemies or lose
Their own; crushed Baghdad, Delhi into dust
For centuries, yet is renowned for skills
And strength; some call him hero, savior,
A "champion of peace"—yes, lies
Can hide in "history" the schoolbooks trust.

That skull-collecting, infant-spearing thug. His fame
Means murder masks its menace with iconic name.

Adviser at the Prince's Ear

They'll try to kill you. Good and nice
Are opposites. Informers guard
Your state of mind. You must reward
Their risks. Yes, feed your lizards mice.

They'll try to kill you. Shrewd means love.
Retreat, and then entrap. Let grin
And frown persuade. Flog, too, and grip
Dissent, but soundproof dungeons. Prove

False accusations. Evidence
Exists for all of them. Again:
Lock, soundproof dungeons. Only then
Could you earn trust. Your lizards tense,

But you stay calm. I must seem cruel—
No more than claws or fangs. Or fist.
We know alternatives exist
If foes kill you, Prince. The eel pool

Means chaos, so be good, not nice.
Prepare to bribe, flog, spy, shoot, slice,
Reward, and love. Power has a price.

Good Luck

—black cat, 13th century A.D.

He meant to fling me on my lady's pyre
To "Burn in hell!" and yet he threw me higher
Than meant, and I, though singed, could sprint and dash
Away, past all that crackling cinder, ash,
And hatred. "Here," they cried, "Grimalkin
Escapes! No, there!" My name is Alcuin,
But now they screeched, "Black devil! Demon! Curse!"
I scampered under thicket into meadow,
Not pausing for a mousy meal, for shadow
Of curiosity, to cry or nurse
My cuts and burns, to bay or pray or plead
Or pout. I ran, I ran, I ran—to edge
Of forest, as if chased along a ledge:
One false step, full stop, half-stop, and I'm dead!
I streaked and sprinted, deeper into green
And brown of forest, and, I think, unseen
By my pursuers, I could slow instead
Of sprint, could start to calibrate my pace,
Could dare to rest, suspire, sniff, and glance
For anyone with hound or sword or lance
Or mace or arrow, dagger, rock. *What place
Is this?* I wondered. Then I sighed, *I breathe!*
My kindest lady's corpse chars, blisters, smokes.
Her soul ascends to heaven. They'll crack jokes
And walnuts, offer prize for me and seethe
That I escaped!
                    And who's the devil? I
Dare wonder. And, more sadly: *Why?*

Hints
—1425 A.D., Europe

You never praise a Turk! You never
Join *Jews* in prayer! And *Waldensians*?!
We'll wind up like the Albigensians!!
Rome snakes this town with spies, with clever
Masks under cowls. Trust *whom*? The clerisy
Accuses cats and bats of heresy!
So much for me as merchant if I mew
Dissent. I wouldn't earn a fishbone. Wife:
Obey. You love the Church, will sip the wine
And swallow wafer, bow to true
Religion. And if a neighbor hints dissension,
Praise Christ and bishops, grin "Oh, all is fine!"

Text
—1490 A.D.

This university could double as a cloister
Where students read (then rampage, drink, and roister).
Theology and rhetoric combined
With ale and romance can enrich the mind
Appealing to divinity. I frolic
And pray. I scroll and stroll, then stray and rollick,
Find God, but not in my text underlined.

"Such Men Are Dangerous"

His subjects prostrate, kneel, implore, and plead
    For his good grace, as if his purple robe
Entails the talent to decide and lead
    Throughout his empire—indeed, the globe.

Prefer a peasant's burlap to silk coat
    And ruby-heavy scepter, razor sword
And temper. Stars, though tiny and remote,
    Sing *God*, not orders I call satrap "Lord."

Statecraft

Around me men see emeralds, diamonds glitter.
I scrub my palace floors and snare stray litter.
They crave harems, dream of midnight orgies.
My wife alone can satisfy my urges.
They sniff dinner fests with fifteen casks of wine,
Pigs filling platters, olives in a sea of brine.
I sip from cup and nibble meat. I'm here
Discussing statecraft with the grand vizier.
They swear to serve (but wait for me to stumble).
I wash the platters, pray I can stay humble.

Feast Fit for a King

With access to our leader's pullies
And levers, I could sic fierce bullies
On enemies, could terrify dissent
To silence and imprison free intent.

I'll savor strawberries instead and sigh
A sonnet, liberate discussion. *Why*
Will foster faithfulness at churches. Priests
Will pray for doubt at conversation's feasts,

Will cherish sassy courtesy, polite
Debate, spiced wine, lunar shine at night.

1765

I

Your rubied crown and ermine robe denote
Great power. Still, your subjects want to vote.

II

You point your golden scepter at dissenter's head
And grumble threats. Consider listening instead.

Citizen of the World

I'm loyal to my veggie garden's soil
Which I can tend because of Arab oil.
I'm loyal to my house, which I can own
Because a Chinese bank helps fund the loan.
I'm loyal to my kids', my city's teams'
Latinos, Asians—All-Stars countless times.
I'm loyal to my people, neighborhood
Of Hernandez, Hansen, Han-Chin: voices heard.

Work to Do

He learns the purpose of a Catholic mission
And racks used by the Spanish Inquisition.
He studies popes' and monarchs' crowning tension
And knows of Carcassone and Albigensian.
He reads of cross debate, the total prism
Of views—and Galileo's prison.
He sees the Lord in stars and seeds and seas
And, too, tsunamis, earthquakes, casualties.
He prays for resolution, pleads for calm,
Knows friends who'd flash a pistol, hum a psalm.

Knowledge

On elevators he won't chat. Who knows
Who's listening. In restaurants, at dinner,
It's golf and basketball, films, who's a winner
And why. It's never business, though. Who knows

Who's listening. His cowl of courtesy
And cross-armed grin hint caution, for who knows
Who's listening. And e-mail, too: who knows
Who watches, reads. He guards each word he'll say

And fences off his trust. That's years away
For best friends. Wife alone he'll kiss, embrace,
But never tell. Who knows? Her trusting face
Could mask. Talk sports, lawns, food? He's social grace,

But business locks his mouth. For wife, a rose
And kiss tonight. And talk of her job, clothes.

Leavings

Stars, Venus silverpoint. Rouge-raspberry
Horizon silhouettes the fading peaks
Above town's distant golden glint, as ferry
Recedes to black, and taillights' scarlet speaks

Far silence, shoreline roads. Commuters sigh,
Then ponder spouses, houses, kids, and bills,
Or how to win the lottery, or why
The supervisor doubts one's office skills,

Or where and when some meeting is tonight,
Or anecdote and punchline. Still, we haul,
Tote, lug, and trek—through poverty, past slight
And injury. We fall and climb and fall

And reach and fall and reach, surmount. We leave
Behind some damage, some accomplishment,
Our books and stories. Those who'll grieve
Might see us on their trail: that distant golden glint.

Suburban Summer Evening

Sun grazes cedar spire through sky's amber heat.
A car approaches from the corner up the street
To hush past forest where the footpaths disappear
To darkness. Cirrus glow of golden-salmon-rose
Burnishes the cedar trunks along suburban road.
Crows jeer the stillness. Dusk blurs snow-tipped peak
To purple shadow. Headlights turn far up the street,
As early porchlights whisper dinnertime and heat.

U District Dusk

Dusk rouge gilds pinnacle of cedar grove
Above a parking lot, its tufted wild grass
Beside graffiti's gripes and giggles
In phosphorescent squiggles
On alley-sided church, stained glass
And sooty brick. Wall preaches x-eyed grins, spray-painted "LOVE."

Protection

That nest at confluence of branches—sticks
And mud on sticks protect beige cheeping chicks,
Whose beaks and claws will soon seem blades and picks.

There—Can You See It?

And birdsong sweetened twenty city streets!
Across a parking lot,
Perched on a roofline—under saffron streaks
Of dawn—one chirping dot.

Chirp

Sun blossoms dawn, on every sector
Of our city pours its golden nectar
As robins chirp green songs next door.

Custodian

A sparrow pecks cream pastry crumbs beneath
An outdoors café chair. How tidy, neat!

Emerging

His risks yield bankruptcy, cold dusks, a cloud
Of isolation, more disputes, a crowd
Of stipulations. Now, he drowses noons
And grouses at his pillow, wishes noose
Or rocket ship to calm. He spurts disdain,
Unshaven candor, blurts his blame again,
Pulls blankets overhead and mumbles. One
O'clock already. Through the blinds, there's sun-
Light. Storms would calm him! Brightness can occlude
His rage, vitality. Yes, better crude
Than phony.
                    Pen on paper, he lets loose!

No Need

Their romance seems a corpse.
He doesn't want an autopsy,
Analysis, apology,
Or detailed record of its course.
He felt their passion wilt. He knows
He wants no funeral, no final rose,
No blaming or remorse,
No final dinner, photo, kiss. No pose.

Shifting Background

No dig or jab or blame. No declamation
Of Bright New Day, denunciation
Of petty fault. No slammed door, sonnets dropped
In trash, gifts smashed—just a friendship stopped
For good reason, without celebration.

Real Place

A frown feels better than a smile
That masks contempt and shines denial.

Whatever

Twenty years ago he would have exploded
At such insults. Now, they're barely noted.
He focuses on tasks, sands and polishes
And hones his work, not wit-stroke that demolishes
A person who'd ignore him anyway to stoke
And irritate. That's all the veil, maya's smoke.

And he forgives himself if he misspoke.

Growing

I keep a stash
Of kindness next to compliments and cash.
I store some generosity by ash
Of disappointment, and my knives I lock
In drawer far from bitterness. I block,
Resist revenge, and yet I keep a stock
Of specs for insight. And I loan them, too.
I've got reserves, and I purchase new.
Speak freely, friends. I'm growing patience now
In fields of study. I've got ground to till,
A mind to irrigate, a heart to fill,
And blades to keep the sharpest when I plow.

Clean-Up

You drop and smash two plates—such clatter!
A hint—your flat holds too much clutter.
Sell books, recycle bottles, donate clothes,
And compost month-old apple, dead-dry rose,
And stew-stained paper plates. It's time to sweep,
Dust, mop, wipe clean. Refresh the place, then sleep
More deeply. And your wall map's decades old.
New wars heat up. Your map's stuck in the Cold.

And yet there's papers piled in *my* place.
Last week I dropped *three* crystal dinner plates
And *then* I swept and scrubbed. I cleansed my nest
But kept a stitched-up coat.
                                          Just do what's best.

Badge of Honor

Adhesive bandage: you now shield, protect
My right big toe from chafing tennis shoe
And fierce bacteria that might infect
Without some antiseptic spray—and *you.*
You help my wound heal, shelter bleeding sore,
Cap scab. Skin knits renewal, as you absorb
Blood stains, pad rawness—save my day, in fact.

Puffs

The hilltop bristles chimneys, evergreens,
And TV towers blinking scarlet dots.
The freeway bisects hill, and traffic knots
Commute. Jet flows through distance, blurs and blots
The urban roar, and yet not these machines
But topaz-turquoise sky, clouds almost still
Puffs, calm and quiet image of the hill
Of scarlet blink and late-day traffic stall.

Blaze

I kindle wick of patience, not the fuse of rage.
Explosions might amuse one's enemies yet hurt
One's friends, so I stay courteous, nix curt
Quip or add compliment. I neither staunch nor cage
Real anger—merely sublimate and channel. Flail,
Flame? Better, listen. Blaze, perhaps, a trail.

The Greatest Battle Scene

His novel's scene-descriptions sang and seared,
And dialogue felt casual yet deep,
So conversational yet unclichéd—
Much better than what I could do. This cheered
And troubled; envy's smirk began to seep
To bloodstream. Jealousy unsheathed its blade
To nick. It stuck its foot out, tried to trip
Another's confidence. But conscience burned
No. Stop the pettiness. This novel's fine,
So learn from it. My ego hid its trap;
I saw, disdained its use and soon returned
To honest praise, light on within the mine
Of convoluted mind. And as I write
I cherish others' skill, not smirk and slight.

Sharp

Let knives chop onions, slice a carrot, spread
Raspberry jelly over whole-grain bread.
Snip tumors, dogmas. Sharpen reason's blade
To purge deceit from eloquence, dread
From honesty. Swords, daggers, yes, can shed
Life's blood. Help tend the orchard, grow the glade.

In midnight's parking lot two youngsters plan
To fight to see which one's the stronger man,
And friends might bring some blades and bullets. Then
Revenge turns fight to feud and friends to clan
Protectors. Peers turn enemies: red, tan,
Black, white, alone or in a pack of ten,

Such hands will stab for honor, valor, friend,
For random fun.
                              Help nurture orchard. Tend.

Aging

I age and tire, slow—yet wonder still.
I want to learn—the lakes of Portugal,
Circumference of the planet Mars, the odes
Of Ancient China and Ben Jonson, roads
Of medieval France, how hugs delight
And why the wife-rejected man will fight
And shoot, why faith in God can curdle, pry
To pettiness and drive out spirit, why
Philosophy needs more than logic to be true,
Why youth explores yet easily explodes
And where besides the earth is life—and who
Will find it, what it is. Age wonders, too,
Can sprint a bit, trust a bit, renew,
And even love—the lakes of Portugal,
Philosophy, and medieval France,
And God, and Shakespeare, love, and dance.

I must set off at once!

Thursday

The countdown to the weekend has begun,
And though a lot of files must be stored
And correspondence typed and copies run
And memos shredded, we approach reward:
Rest, fun, the rites that stimulate accord
At barbeque or ball game, carnival
Or synagogue or cinema or church,
At picnic table, gallery, or mall,
For shoppers, worshippers, and all who search
Their blood for sky, their hope for pulse, the stars
For stories, music for a God, true love
For celebration healing break-up scars,
A fountain thrusting frothy blobs aloft
In praise. Remember that—when bitter, bored.

Saturday

It's after sleep. I lie in bed at noon,
Reposing in the stillness, blood-warmth, calm.
Through slats I sense the sun but love this balm
Of pillows, blankets. I let silence croon
My pulse and won't enforce awareness. Work
Today means errands, not the dash to bus
And office tower, not the rush and fuss
Of deadlined goals. I lounge in leisure, perk
Enough to finish tasks, then write and think
And stroll. Soon, afternoon withdraws for streaks
Of opal-auburn over bay and streets
Defined by lamps and signs. Stars, planets prink
The evening. Body sighs, rebalances.
Atop the bay, lamps rest their shiny lances.

To Tact

The ferry dreams along moon-whispered waves
    To harbor past the island crest
And slides from sight. Its wake
    Disperses in the bay, its nest

Of lamps aglitter, yet dimin-
    ishing. Now, Venus brightens peach
Horizon, and the stars begin
    To signal distance, nighttime's beach.

I settle, soften, glad that tact
    Today let me converse without
Declaring fight, denying fact,
    Or denigrating those who doubt.

Tides: in and out and in and out.
I asked, decided, didn't shout.

Cramming Calm

I sprint, I scream—and catch my bus
And dash to office desk on time.
I breakfast: two Excedrin Plus
And cup of sugared java, tie
And schedule tight. I cannot calm
The phone. I mumble, "Lord, I need
Your help" at bathroom mirror, comb
My hair, rinse hands, my heart a steed
That gallops through my blood. My tasks
Breed, multiply, divide. Subtract
A few, and still I grow keen tusks
And hooves to battle through each fact
And phony, list and lie and lapse.
Excedrin three and four. Ten dollars
Buys thirty-minute sandwich, minute naps.
My calendar appointment hollers
Two. Lord, I need Your help. And friend,

I need yours, too.

Survival

Despite the fog, cars, buses cruise across
Steel bridge—appointments, errands, and delays
Await like lamps that pierce penumbral haze.
Already, second pot of Starbucks brews.
Discussions percolate with weekends, news,
The home team's playoff-ousting one-point loss,
Lunch plans for Tuesday noon, and how the boss
Insists you finish that agenda
Soon…back to work. Swirl creamer, Splenda,
And respite into coffee mug, and toss
Hot raisin bagel halves on paper plate,
Stride back to keyboard, and accelerate
Your typing hands. Through fog and fear and fret
We fight to finish tasks, to bear the freight
Of haste and worry. Your reward?—you keep
Your job, ride bus, pay rent, and safely sleep

And write or paint or sculpt or sing and dance
Across a week. At work, you water plants.

Business World

The freeway entrance ramps begin to crowd
Beneath scarred charcoal peach, magenta-browed.
A contrail fluffs into a cirrus cloud,
A track across horizon. Day is long
As night, and batters us with chore. Yet, song
Can soothe and jokes delight, and wrong
Can help us learn what's right. We drive up ramps,
The city trading sequins for its office lamps,
For suit or slacks, its whisper for its amps.

Haze vanishes, and deadlines challenge rush
Through golden turquoise morning. Day is long
As night. I sing and joke, as well as run.

Blame

Let right blame left and left blame right,
And center blame them both. The truth
Defies all labels yet persists
Through complicated moments, mists
And segues, morphs and blends. One slight
Mistake might loosen bolts on jet
And yield a crash and kill the troops
And many villagers, whole groups
Of center, left, and right. One jot,
One dust mote could crash hard drive, might
Confuse, upset, destroy machine,
Defy a label shouting "Clean."
Pause, ponder, ask, revise, review.
Jobs, hard drives, friendships crash, and you
Might die, no matter who's to blame.

Quake

—*after two earthquakes, 2010*

So, nature jerks her tablecloth from underneath
The plates again. In Haiti, Chile: death,
Parched throats and empty stomachs, fever, dust, and debt.
Pray, yes—for cash, construction skill. Then offer wreath.
Perhaps God sees and hears. Perhaps It's blind and deaf.
Fair deal? Can arguing the call persuade the ref?

Aftershock

*—of fraudulent charities
for earthquake victims*

An earthquake jolts, and a tsunami
Slams half our city to salami
And mulch, and you scam donors, sweet talk trust
To sucker for your scam. Your heart's a crust,
A shell, and you don't care. An earthquake
To you means cash. You swindle loot, your take.

I pray some aftershock jolts you awake.

Nature

Volcanoes, earthquakes don't mean nature's evil—
Yet such destruction and upheaval!
And sunlight, roses don't mean nature's warm—
Yet, how refreshing after a storm!

Downtown Gull

I

You cruise
Horizon's fifty opal blues
And drift a sinking circle. Then you ride
An updraft, wings above the water, glide
Your leisure over bay and boulevard
And float a blade of dream. You swim the air
In leisure groove. Below: the stoplight rush,
Migrations over bridges, crush
Of crowds. But we'll return at dawn, and I
Again will see you liberate our sky.

II

How kind of people to provide
These palaces past which I glide,
Careen, and cruise all day!
Through wide gray sunshine, dreamy clouds,
I scamper over traffic, crowds,
And bay. I fish and loop and play!

Fire

I twirl past fires, on a tightrope, on
A ledge, across the rapids, stone by stone,
Aware a heart ignited by a kiss
Can, scorned, despise and scorch and hiss.
I step through minefield so serene near road
And orchard, yet...I know it could explode.

A heart ignited by a kiss might blaze
To love, then smolder into smoke and haze.

I twirl past fires, try to nurse one past the dawn.

The Villager Considers

Let's say we build the bridge. It brings
Trade, merchants, thieves, musicians
And murderers, gold and diamond rings,
Silks, swords, salt, cinnamon, munitions,
Friends braving stony paths and spies
And soldiers, holiness and horror, hope
And blood. A bridge means trust when lies
Prevail, and yet how else can truth grow whole,
Can aspiration learn? Let's say we build
This bridge to life beyond us: the unknown.
Then ask: does God want us to stay alone?
Are we alone? No. Celebrate, then, guild
And choir, visitors. Find, fit stone, brick.
Then welcome sword sheath, handshake, walking stick.

David D. Horowitz founded and manages Rose Alley Press. His previous poetry collections include *Stars Beyond the Battlesmoke*; *Wildfire, Candleflame*; *Resin from the Rain*; and *Streetlamp, Treetop, Star*. His poems have been published in numerous journals, including *The Lyric*, *Candelabrum*, and *The New Formalist*, and his essays often appear in *Exterminating Angel*. He lives and works in Seattle, where he frequently organizes and performs at readings. His website is www.rosealleypress.com.

Photograph by Ed Goralnick

Other *Rose Alley Press Titles*

Caruso for the Children, & Other Poems by William Dunlop, 978-0-9651210-2-6, paper, $9.95
"Dunlop is a brilliant metrical technician…. richly allusive, a gifted parodist." —Jonathan Raban

Rain Psalm, poems by Victoria Ford, 978-0-9651210-0-2, paper, $5.95
"Victoria Ford's poems are at once modest and courageous, cut clean and sure…" —Sam Hamill

From Notebook to Bookshelf: Writing, Publishing, & Marketing Basics to Get Your Writing Read
by David D. Horowitz, 978-0-9745024-6-5, velo, $5.95
"*From Notebook to Bookshelf* is a great resource for my students." —Holly Hughes

Resin from the Rain, poems by David D. Horowitz, 978-0-9651210-8-8, paper, $9.95
"The office worker's plight, the murder in the papers, the lonely streetwalker at dusk all find
residence in Horowitz's humanity." —Derek Sheffield

Stars Beyond the Battlesmoke by David D. Horowitz, 978-0-9745024-7-2, paper, $9.95
"*Stars Beyond the Battlesmoke* is filled with memorable lines, keen observations, and acute wit."
—Lana Hechtman Ayers

Streetlamp, Treetop, Star, poems by David D. Horowitz, 978-0-9651210-5-7, paper, $9.95
"…an excellent new book—'words…to cleanse even the sharpest wounds.'" —Carol Robertshaw

Strength & Sympathy: Essays & Epigrams by David D. Horowitz, 978-0-9651210-1-9, paper, $8.95
"…incisive essays and epigrams that take us from proper pronouns to considerate theology."
—Mícéál F. Vaughan

Wildfire, Candleflame, poems by David D. Horowitz, 978-0-9745024-3-4, paper, $9.95
"What a joy it is to read formal verse written by one who has mastered his craft." —Sharon E. Svendsen

Limbs of the Pine, Peaks of the Range: Poems by Twenty-Six Pacific Northwest Poets,
edited by David D. Horowitz, 978-0-9745024-4-1, paper, $12.95
"This anthology offers truth at every turn." —Terry Martin

Many Trails to the Summit: Poems by Forty-Two Pacific Northwest Poets, edited by David D. Horowitz,
978-0-9745024-8-9, paper, $14.95. "What a joy it is to read poems that are coherent, musical,
funny, dramatic, surprising, and just plain beautiful." —Sharon Cumberland

On Paper Wings, poems by Donald Kentop, 978-0-9745024-0-3, paper, $6.95
"Donald Kentop writes with an assurance that invites the reader into his poems…. This is an
accomplished and memorable collection." —Richard Wakefield

To Enter the Stillness, poems by Douglas Schuder, 978-0-9651210-7-1, paper, $6.95
"Douglas Schuder brings uncommonly graceful phrasing to everything he sees." —David Mason

Adam Chooses, poems by Michael Spence, 978-0-9651210-4-0, paper, $9.95.
"…elegant design and formal ease we've come to expect of Spence's work." —Madeline DeFrees

Weathered Steps, poems by Joannie Kervran Stangeland, 978-0-9651210-9-5, paper, $6.95
"*Weathered Steps* is a book about all that you almost don't notice, but should." —Melinda Mueller

Rose Alley Press
www.rosealleypress.com